Winter Whispers:

Poems for Winter Days

Karima Ameziani

DEDICATION

To you, winter wanderers and seekers of solace, In snow's quiet marvels, finding a place. This book, an offering for your frost-kissed nights, Where tales of winter's embrace take flight.

May its verses stir fires in your wintry soul, Embracing frost's allure, making you whole. Discover in each page, the season's tender art, A world of snow-kissed dreams, to warmly impart.

With heartfelt gratitude, it's shared with you, To immerse in winter's wonder, anew. Let each line weave a tale of cozy delight, As you journey through winter's enchanting night.

CONTENTS

Introduction

Dear Reader,

I must confess, I am not a poet. Yet, there are moments when nature's beauty and the magic of winter have stirred something within me. "Winter Whispers" is a humble attempt to capture the fleeting moments and quiet musings that the frost-kissed season has gifted me.

Sitting by the frosted window, watching snowflakes weave intricate patterns in the air, I found myself drawn to the subtle poetry of nature. The laughter of children building snowmen, the aroma of freshly brewed cocoa, and the comforting crackle of logs in the fireplace all found their way into these verses.

I invite you to indulge in these winter whispers, whether it's by reading a few lines before bed to embrace the tranquil spirit of the season, or savoring them with a morning coffee to start your day with a deeper connection to winter's embrace. Feel free to dive into these pages anytime you seek a moment of reflection or a touch of the wintry aesthetic.

These poems are a reflection of my heartfelt attempt to express the profound connection I feel with the wintry world. It is my hope that through these simple lines, you too can experience the tender beauty and introspective solace that winter has graciously bestowed upon me.

With genuine warmth and an amateur's pen,

Welcome to "Winter Whispers: Poems for Winter Days."

Hello Winter

As autumn ends its whispering tale,

Leaves of amber and crimson start to pale.

Nature's rhythm shifts, the air turns cool,

As winter waits, patient, in its quiet rule.

Hello, Winter, in your crisp embrace,

Veiled in whispers, a tranquil grace.

Leaves surrender, their fiery hues fade,

As you blanket the world in a soft, cool cascade.

Snowflake Serenade

Snowflakes gently pirouette,

In the hush of winter's set.

A serenade of icy lace,

Softly whispering in their grace.

In the stillness of the night,

Each flake glows in pure white.

A symphony of frosty light,

Guiding the world through wintry night.

Winter's Embrace

In winter's silent embrace,

Behold, nature's wonderland, Serene and cold.

Where snowflakes dance in the crisp air,

And frosty branches glisten, Oh so fair.

The earth, in white,

wears a sparkling gown,

a landscape of Enchantment all around.

With every step, a soft crunch and creak

A symphony of stillness,

Tranquil and meek

Beyond Christmas

Beyond the festive cheer and yuletide tales,

In winter's quiet grace, a deeper journey unveils.

Where the heart seeks solace and the soul finds

reprieve, In the gentle hush of snow,

we learn to believe.

Beyond the merriment and the joyous chimes,

Winter's embrace beckons, transcending times.

It's in the quiet moments, where life finds its rhyme,

Where the spirit finds solace,

for now, and all time.

Winter Home

In the nook of the cottage,

by the hearth's warm embrace,

A symphony of comfort, a haven of grace.

Where flickering flames paint shadows on the walls,

And the coziness within, a cherished embrace that

enthralls.

In this winter retreat, let the spirit find its ease,

Where the world outside fades, and the soul finds its

peace. Embraced by the cottage's warmth,

in this silent retreat, we find solace and comfort,

life's most tender treat.

Winter Tales

Softly, the snow whispers tales untold,

A dance of delicate flakes, a sight to behold.

In each icy crystal, a world in miniature,

A wonderland unfolds, pure and sure.

With every step, the snow crunches and sings,

A melody of winter, on gossamer wings.

Embracing the chill, the world becomes still,

As whispers of snow, the heart does fill.

Winter Kitchen

In the simmering pot, a tale of winter brews,

A symphony of flavors, a delightful muse.

From mulled spices to savory stews,

Winter's warmth resides in each hearty chew.

With every sip of cocoa, a moment to savor,

A hug from within, a delightful favor.

In the aroma of spices, a dance of the senses,

The taste of winter's warmth,

A gift that commences.

Winter's Wisdom

In the gentle hush of winter, nature's pace reveals,

Life's lesson in slowing, its rhythm gently appeals.

From the stillness of snowfall to the patience of ice,

Winter whispers softly, teaching us to be wise.

With every snowflake's descent, a call to pause,

To embrace the quiet, to live without cause.

In the dormant landscapes, a lesson in rest,

What winter teaches us, is to be at our best.

Whispers of winter

In the whispers of winter's breath,

Secrets of frost are softly kept.

A tale of snowflakes' silent flight,

Painting the world in purest white.

Amidst the chill, a quiet refrain,

As nature sleeps beneath its chain.

Whispers carry the season's tune,

Beneath the glow of the silent moon.

Winter Moon

Beneath the moon's ethereal light,

Nature sleeps, blanketed in white.

In winter's chilly, yet tender hold,

Each moment glistens, pure and bold.

Frosty tendrils caress the air,

Embracing all with a delicate flair.

A touch of chill, a kiss of grace,

In winter's loving, frosty embrace.

Icy Reverie

Icy dreams in winter's keep,

Where snow and frost gently seep.

In reverie's chill, a world so bright,

A dance of frost in the pale moonlight.

Thoughts freeze in the wintry air,

In a realm where frost lays bare.

An icy reverie, a frozen flight,

Embracing the world in crystal delight.

Winter's Lullaby

In the stillness of winter's night,
Hear the lullaby of snow so light.
A melody woven in frosty air,
A soothing hum beyond compare.

Snowflakes whisper, a gentle croon,
Underneath the glowing, wintry moon.
Winter's lullaby, a tender sight,
Guiding the world through the tranquil night.

Arctic Dreams

In the land of Arctic dreams,
Where frost reigns and silence gleams.
Visions of ice and snow entwine,
In a world where chill defines.

Polar fantasies in the frozen night,
Painting the world in hues so bright.
Arctic dreams, a frigid sight,
Guiding the world through the winter's might.

Frozen Symphony

In winter's symphony, a frozen array,
Where snowflakes dance in silent ballet.
A harmony of ice and frost so bright,
Painting the world in hues of white.

Melodies of snow in the wintry air,
Weaving a tune beyond compare.
A frozen symphony, a pristine delight,
Guiding the world through the frosty night.

Solstice Shadows

In the solstice's quiet shadows deep,
Where wintry secrets softly sleep.
A dance of darkness, a touch of light,
In the longest of winter's night.

Shadows whisper in the frosty air,
Tales of solstice, rare and fair.
Solstice shadows, a mystical sight,
Guiding the world through the wintry night.

The Snow Queen's Tale

In the Snow Queen's icy domain,
Frosty stories softly reign.
A tale of winter's chilling grace,
Woven in snowflakes' delicate embrace.

A regal frost in the wintry night,
A dance of ice, a shimmering sight.
The Snow Queen's tale, a frosty trail,
Guiding the world through the winter's veil.

Crystal Silence

In the crystal silence of winter's keep,

Where snow and frost gently sleep.

A world of hush, of quiet delight,

Embracing the world in tranquil white.

Silence weaves through the frosty air,

A tranquil peace beyond compare.

Crystal silence, a serene respite,

Guiding the world through the tranquil night.

Blizzard Ballad

In the blizzard's wild and swirling flight,
A ballad of snow in the wintry night.
A symphony of ice and howling air,
Painting the world in a frosty glare.

Melodies of snow in the tempest's might,
Weaving a tune both fierce and light.
Blizzard ballad, a tempestuous sight,
As nature's power dances through the night.

Enchanted Frost

Within the realm of enchanted frost,
Where winter's touch is softly embossed.
A dance of ice and snow so rare,
In a world where magic fills the air.

Whispers weave through the frosty air,
A spellbinding tale beyond compare.
Enchanted frost, a mystical light,
As nature's wonders come into sight.

A Winter's Palette

Upon winter's canvas, a painter's delight,
Hues of frost and snow so pure and white.
A palette of ice and delicate hue,
Crafting a world both timeless and new.

Colors whisper in the wintry air,
A masterpiece beyond compare.
A winter's palette, a vision so bright,
In every stroke, revealing nature's might.

Fireside Tales

By the fireside's comforting glow,
Where embers dance and shadows grow,
Tales of winters long ago unfold,
Their magic stories, timeless and bold.

In the crackling fire's golden light,
Imagination takes its flight,
Painting scenes of frost-kissed lore,
Entwined with the hearth's warm rapport.

Each flickering flame, a storyteller's art,
Weaving dreams in every heart,
Embracing all in its enchanting hold,
As winter's mysteries are gently told.

Whispering Wind Chimes

Beneath the wintry sky's expanse,
Where snowflakes twirl in a graceful dance,
The whispering wind chimes softly sing,
Their melodies through the frosty air ring.

Each gentle note, a tale untold,
Of winters past and stories bold,
Echoing through the silent night,
Guiding hearts to a tranquil sight.

Their harmonies weave a soothing spell,
In the icy breeze, they gently dwell,
A symphony of peace in the frost's embrace,
A timeless melody, a whispering grace.

Frozen Echoes

In the land of frozen echoes deep,

Where winters whisper and secrets keep,

Echoes of snowflakes softly sleep,

A symphony of frost in silence, so steep.

Whispers of tales from winters of yore,

Stories that drift from forevermore,

Mysteries woven in the wintry air,

Echoing tales of frost so fair.

Each frozen echo, a memory's trace,

In the stillness of this wintry place,

A chorus of ice in the silent air,

Taking the world through the cold's despair.

Aurora Borealis Ballad

In the dance of the Aurora's vivid hue,
A ballad of colors in the wintry view,
Celestial brushstrokes painting the sky,
A cosmic masterpiece soaring high.

A symphony of hues in the dark expanse,
Whispering secrets of the cosmic dance,
With every shimmer, a tale of the night,
Embracing the magic of the dark's flight.

Winter Wonderland Waltz

In the winter wonderland's pristine white,
Where snowflakes waltz in the soft moonlight,
A delicate choreography, a dance so rare,
Embracing the world in an ethereal affair.

Amidst the tranquil hush of the snow,
Nature orchestrates a mesmerizing show,
Each flake a dancer, graceful and light,
Weaving a tale of the wintry night.

Crystalline Cascade

A cascade of crystals in the frozen air,
Frosty wonders woven with tender care,
Each snowflake a masterpiece, delicate and bright,
A shimmering spectacle, pure and light.

In the wintry landscape's silent grace,
Nature unveils its crystalline embrace,
A mesmerizing sight, enchanting and grand,
Crafting a vision so intricately planned.

The cascade descends with a gentle grace,
A dance of frost in the open space,
A tale of winter's artistry, pure and wide,
Reflecting the magic of nature's pride.

Snowy Symphony

Beneath the silent sky's snowy expanse,

A symphony of snowflakes begins to dance,

In the hushed night, each flake takes flight,

Weaving a melody of winter's delight.

The soft descent, a delicate refrain,

A timeless tune of frost's gentle reign,

Each snowflake, a note in the wintry air,

Crafting a symphony beyond compare.

The world listens in the frost's embrace,

As nature paints with delicate grace,

A snowy symphony, a masterpiece so bright,

Bringing the magic of winter to light.

Snowbound Sonata

In the snowbound landscape's pristine embrace,
Nature orchestrates a sonata with grace,
Snowflakes twirl and dance in the frosty air,
Weaving a melody beyond compare.

Each delicate note, a tale of the cold,
A symphony of winter's story unfolds,
The world listens in the tranquil night,
Enchanted by the snow's whispered delight.

Glacial Garland

Amidst the icy expanse of winter's domain,
A glacial garland weaves a frosty refrain,
Each crystalline thread, a story of the cold,
Crafting a vision both wondrous and bold.

In the quiet glimmer of the frost-kissed night,
Nature adorns the world with shimmering light,
A garland of ice in the wintry air,
Reflecting the beauty that's found everywhere.

The glacial garland adorns the land with grace,
A testament to winter's delicate embrace,
Capturing the magic of the frost's grandeur,
Enchanting the world with its crystalline allure.

Snow Fog

In the hush of winter's silent breath,
A veil of fog descends, embracing the earth.
Soft tendrils of mist, an ethereal shroud,
Wrap the world in a tranquil, muted cloud.

Amidst the ghostly whispers that gently play,
Nature cloaks herself in a mystical display.
A dance of opacity, a sight surreal,
Where the boundaries blur, and senses feel.

Through the enigmatic haze, shadows roam,
Mysteries unfold in the fog's embrace, at home.
A serene enchantment, veiled and still,
Winter's fog weaves a moment, tranquil and chill.

New Year's Eve

Beneath the winter's glittering sky,
New Year's Eve draws nigh.
A hush befalls the snowy scene,
As the old year gracefully convenes.

Frosty whispers fill the air,
Echoing dreams of hope and care.
In the chill of the wintry night,
Resolutions dance in the starry light.

Amidst the shimmer of snow's embrace,
Hearts alight with dreams to chase.
A moment to reflect, to renew,
As the countdown begins, anew.

With each snowflake's gentle descent,
Anticipation hums, quietly intent.
In the winter's embrace, a promise gleams,
Welcoming the dawn of new dreams.

Hello December

Hello, December, with your whispered sigh,
You tiptoe in, under the frosty sky.
A time for tales spun in silver and gold,
As winter's secrets begin to unfold.

With every snowflake's delicate descent,
You paint the world in wonderment.
The hush of your arrival, a symphony in white,
As nature's whispers ignite the night.

The aroma of cinnamon and evergreen,
Serenades the senses, a nostalgic scene.
Hello, December, with your spirited grace,
You weave enchantment in every place.

In the cradle of your quiet embrace,
Fireside dreams find their perfect space.
Hello, December, with your stories to tell,
In your embrace, we find a timeless spell.

Northern Nectar

In the realm where winter's touch is bold,
Northern nectar weaves its tales untold.
A sip of magic from the frost-kissed air,
A potion brewed with nature's tender care.

Beneath the dancing auroras' gentle light,
Northern nectar flows, pure and bright.
A symphony of sweetness in the chill,
Where wintry wonders hum and thrill.

January's Breath

In January's breath, the world stands still,
As frosty whispers blanket every hill.
A tapestry of snow and icy lace,
Weaving tales of a tranquil embrace.

The air, crisp and clear, with a wintry bite,
Nature's symphony plays in the pale sunlight.
A dance of frost in the silent morn,
As January's weather gracefully adorns.

Through the chilly days and starlit nights,
The season's magic paints the land in white.
In the quietude of January's serene air,
Moments of stillness find solace there.

The Wintery Farm

The barn stands steadfast, in the pale morning light,
A sentinel of life, in the stillness of night.
Where echoes of seasons past linger in the air,
Embracing the land with a tender, timeless care.

In the orchard's embrace, the trees stand tall,
Their boughs adorned with a snowy shawl.
Dreams of harvests to come silently stir,
In the soul of the winter, a hope does confer.

Through the snow-laden fields,
A quiet resilience prevails,
Where the heart of the farm humbly unveils.
In the depth of the winter's serene charm,
The spirit of the land finds peace and calm.

Snow Angels

Children frolic in the glistening snow,

Crafting angels with hearts all aglow.

Their laughter echoes in the frosty air,

As they lay down with a tender care,

Their silhouettes etched in the powdery white,

A testament to innocence, pure and bright.

Each delicate form, a heavenly sight,

In the wintry landscape, a moment so right,

As the snow angels rest with grace untold,

Their presence a story of joy to unfold.

Winter Birds

Amidst the winter's hush and icy cold,
Snow birds take flight, brave and bold.
Their wings adorned with the frost's embrace,
Navigating the chill with elegant grace.

In the crisp, clear sky, they paint a scene,
A dance of resilience, serene and keen.
A symphony of feathers in the wintry light,
Guiding the world through the frosty night.

Each snow bird's call, a melody so clear,
A message of hope in the cold frontier.
In the vast expanse of the snowy morn,
Their presence a testament, quietly born.

Winter Trees

Silhouettes etched against the pale sky,

Winter trees whisper tales of days gone by.

A dance of shadows in the cold light,

Echoing the mysteries of day and night.

In their stoic repose, they hold a story,

Of resilience and strength, in all their glory.

Roots intertwined in the frozen ground,

An ode to endurance, profound and sound.

Through the whispers of the frosty breeze,

Winter trees stand tall, adorned with ease.

In the heart of the season's quiet spree,

They embody nature's timeless decree.

Christmas Spirit

Amidst the winter's gentle, snowy spread,

The Christmas spirit awakens, lightly treads.

A symphony of joy in the frosty air,

Weaving a tale of love and care.

In the twinkle of lights and the evergreen,

The Christmas spirit dances, bright and keen.

A melody of giving, of hearts aglow,

Embracing the world with a tranquil flow.

Through the laughter and the cherished cheer,

The Christmas spirit whispers, crystal clear.

A timeless embrace, a message of peace,

Filling every moment, never to cease.

In the soul of the season, it finds its place,

The Christmas spirit, a guiding grace.

A reminder of hope and love's pure art,

Enveloping the world, touching every heart

Serene Nights

In the hush of winter's deep repose,
The night unfolds in a frost-kissed pose.
Stars shimmer in the cold, dark expanse,
A celestial dance, a cosmic trance.

The moon casts a glow, serene and bright,
Guiding the world through the wintry night.
Silence weaves through the frost-laden air,
Embracing the land with a tranquil flair.

Through the stillness, a whispering breeze,
Carries the secrets of ancient trees.
In the quiet embrace of the night's embrace,
Winter's enchantment finds its place.

Winter's breath

In the stillness of the wintry morn,

Winter's breath whispers, softly born.

A gentle chill in the frost-laced air,

A tender touch, beyond compare.

Through the barren trees, it softly sighs,

Painting the world with a quiet disguise.

Each exhale, a tale of ice and lace,

Enveloping the land in a delicate embrace.

In the essence of its touch, a moment to behold,

Winter's breath weaves a tale, timeless and cold.

A reminder of nature's beauty and depth,

In every sigh of winter's breath.

Windows In Winter

In the quiet of the wintry scene,

Windows frame a world serene.

A portal to vistas, far and near,

Where stories whisper, crystal clear.

Through the frosty glass, a view unfolds,

A glimpse of tales waiting to be told.

In each pane, a reflection of light,

A dance of shadows, both day and night.

In the warmth of the room, windows embrace,

The outside world with a gentle grace.

A barrier between, yet a bridge to explore,

A connection to lands, both less and more.

Enchanting February

In the hush of February's fleeting breath,

A whisper of enchantment, silent and fresh.

A tapestry of moments in the winter's hold,

Where mysteries linger and tales unfold.

Amidst the wintry scene, a subtle shift,

As nature's hand bestows a special gift.

The snowflakes, they fall in a dance so rare,

Painting the earth with a delicate flair.

The Snowman Pooti

In the heart of the winter's snowy embrace,

Stood Pooti, a snowman with a friendly face.

Buttons for eyes and a smile so wide,

Pooti stood tall with arms open wide.

His carrot nose pointed toward the sky,

In the chilly breeze, he stood tall and spry.

A hat made of snow adorned his head,

As he watched over the land with a snowy spread.

Children would gather, their laughter would ring,

As they adorned Pooti with a scarf and a string.

With each passing day, he would never complain,

Upon the earth's serene and wintry repose,

Nature lays down a blanket of shimmering snow.

A soft embrace, in the season's quiet spread,

Wintery Bed

Cradling the land in a tranquil winter bed.

Beneath the snowy quilt, the world finds rest,
Dreaming of the spring's gentle caress.
In the stillness of slumber, a dormant grace,
Awaiting the awakening of nature's embrace.

The trees stand sentinel, in their icy attire,
As the winter bed holds the land in its quiet mire.
Echoes of life and the promise of rebirth,
Linger softly in the frozen earth.

Winter's sun

In the quiet realm of the winter's reign,

The sun peeks through the frosty pane.

A golden kiss on the snow-laden ground,

A touch of warmth in the stillness found.

Through the icy haze and the frost's embrace,

The winter's sun paints a gentle grace.

A subtle glow in the crisp, cold air,

A reminder of light, serene and rare.

In the heart of the season's tranquil hold,

The sun's gentle rays weave stories untold.

A dance of shadows, in the snow's delight,

A fleeting warmth in the wintry night.

Changing Constellations

In the vast expanse where stars align,
Changing constellations gracefully entwine.
Their ancient dance across the wintry night,
Painting tales of wonder in celestial light.

Through the frost-kissed air and the stillness deep,
Changing constellations their secrets keep.
A symphony of patterns, a cosmic display,
Guiding the world along its timeless way.

Each shimmering point, a story to unfold,
In the shifting tapestry of the night's hold.
As seasons pass and moments fade,
Changing constellations their stories pervade.

Supper in Winter

In the heart of the winter's frosty domain,

Nature offers a feast in its wintry terrain.

Roots and tubers hidden in the frozen ground,

Nurtured by the earth, waiting to be found.

Apples and pears from the autumn's yield,

Stored with care, a winter's bounty sealed.

Their sweetness preserved in the chilly air,

A reminder of harvest, both humble and fair.

Berries, frozen in time, a vibrant hue,

Nature's jewels glistening, pure and true.

Their tangy essence captured in icy sheen,

A taste of summer in the wintry scene.

Ice Skates

Beneath the winter's glistening sheen,

Ice skates glide, the world serene.

Blades carve a tale on the frozen floor,

A dance of elegance, an icy allure.

In the crisp, cold air, a melody resounds,

As skaters twirl and the ice surrounds.

A symphony of motion, both swift and light,

Gracefully painting the wintry night.

Laces tied, snug and secure,

Ice skates whisper, their stories endure.

Of gliding dreams and the frost's embrace,

Enchanting the world with their timeless grace.

Winter's Cloak

In the quiet of the wintry night's embrace,

Winter's cloak drapes the earth with grace.

A garment of snow, soft and pristine,

Enfolding the world in a tranquil sheen.

Underneath its folds, the land lies still,

Awaiting the touch of spring's gentle thrill.

A hushed repose in the frost's delight,

As winter's cloak blankets the earth in white.

Through its icy veil, a hushed symphony,

Nature whispers secrets, both wild and free.

A tale of slumber in the wintry air,

Enveloping the world with a tender care.

Autumn to Winter

As the vibrant colors of autumn fade and wane,
A whispered message lingers for winter's reign.
Leaves rustle gently, sharing tales of old,
Passing on wisdom, adorned in red and gold.

With a gentle sigh, autumn conveys its plea,
To winter, the bearer of frost and glee.
A tale of beauty and letting go,
A reminder of life's ebb and flow.

In the quietude of the changing scene,
Autumn's message echoes, both bold and serene.
A passing of the torch, in nature's timeless way,
Embracing the cycle with each passing day.

In the heart of the shift, a bond is formed,
As autumn and winter, in harmony, performed.
A seamless transition, a story unfurled,
As nature weaves the tapestry of the world.

Chimney Smoke

Amidst the wintry chill, a chimney's smoke,
Rising gently, in a delicate evoke.
A trail of warmth against the frosty air,
Weaving tales of comfort, beyond compare.

Whispers of hearthside tales in the gentle plume,
Curling and swirling, in the wintry gloom.
A dance of embers, in the chimney's flight,
Painting the sky with a cozy light.

In the heart of the winter's serene hold,
Chimney smoke weaves stories, both brave and
bold.
A comforting presence, in the frost's embrace,
Guiding the world with its familiar grace.

Winter Storms

In the wintry expanse, where the wind does blow,
Storms of snow whirl, in a mystical show.
A dance of flakes, in the chilly air,
Creating a spectacle, beyond compare.

The world is cloaked in a blanket of white,
As storms of snow weave a tale, pure and bright.
Nature's fury, with a gentle grace,
Enveloping the earth in its icy embrace.

Through the gusts and the flurry, a symphony sings,
As storms of snow reveal nature's wild wings.
A hushed beauty in the wintry sight,
Guiding the world through the blizzard's might.

The Winter Sky

Where winter's touch graces the night and day,
Sunsets paint the skies in a vibrant display.
Hues of pink and orange, a celestial fire,
Illuminating the world with a tranquil desire.
As dawn breaks, in the wintry hush,
Sunrises whisper, painting the world in a blush.
A palette of gold and blue, a breathtaking sight,
Easing the transition from dark to light.

The sun's gentle rays kiss the frost-laden ground,
Infusing the landscape with warmth profound.
A symphony of colors, both gentle and bold,
Guiding the world through the wintry cold.
In the heart of the day's transition,
A beauty prevails,
As winter sunsets and sunrises unveil their tales.
A celestial dance, both radiant and wise,
Enlivening the spirit, beneath the wintry skies.

The frozen lake

Beneath the winter's hush, a frozen lake,
Still and serene, in its icy embrace.
Reflections of the sky, tranquil and clear,
A mirrored world, devoid of fear.

Silent ripples frozen in time,
A testament to the season's icy rhyme.
Nature's stillness, in the cold air,
A frozen moment, both stark and fair.

In the heart of the frozen lake's repose,
Nature's beauty in its wintry pose.
A portrait of tranquility, both bold and bright,
Guiding the world through the wintry night.

Winter's Kitchen Symphony

In the heart of the winter's embrace,
The kitchen hums with a familiar grace.
Pots and pans orchestrate a symphony sweet,
A melody of warmth and flavors to greet.

Spices dance in the wintry air,
Aromas weave tales, beyond compare.
Cinnamon and nutmeg in the frost's delight,
Infusing the kitchen with a cozy light.
Vegetables simmer in a hearty stew,
Nature's bounty cooked with love anew.
Their vibrant colors swirl in the pot,
Creating a tapestry, a savory plot.

Baking dough rises, a promise of delight,
Filling the kitchen with aromas so bright.
Cookies and pies in the oven's warm hold,
Crafting a tale of winter's sweet gold.

Solitude Of Winter

Within the winter's grasp, where silence holds sway,
Solitude whispers, freeing the chains.
A tranquil hush in the frost-kissed air,
Embracing the soul with a tender care.

Footprints in the snow, the only trace,
Of a solitary journey, a gentle pace.
Nature's stillness, in the wintry scene,
A timeless moment, both stark and serene.

In the heart of the solitude's tender hold,
Winter's embrace weaves stories untold.
A sanctuary of calm, in the frost's domain,
Nurturing the spirit with a quiet refrain.

Winter Twilight

In the waning light of the winter's embrace,
Twilight descends with a gentle grace.
Shadows lengthen, the world grows still,
A quietude settles over the wintry hill.

Hints of gold blend with shades of blue,
As daylight fades, and night ensues.
A symphony of colors, soft and profound,
Enveloping the earth without a sound.

In the heart of the twilight's tranquil hold,
Winter's essence weaves stories, bold and old.
A moment of reflection, in nature's design,
Embracing the world as day resigns.

Holidays' Delight

In the glow of the holiday's cheerful light,
Delight doth dance freely, merry and bright.
Laughter doth echo in the frosty air,
As joy and merriment doth grace everywhere.

Families gather 'round the hearth's warm flame,
Sharing stories and love, each one the same.
The aroma of feasts, a tantalizing sight,
Filling the air with a festive delight.

Children's laughter doth ring with glee,
As they unwrap gifts beneath the wintry tree.
Thine eyes do sparkle with wonder, thine heart full
and gay,
Embracing the magic of the holiday.

Snow-covered Rooftops

Upon the rooftops, a blanket of snow,

Rests gently, in the winter's soft glow.

A hushed repose in the frosty air,

A tranquil scene, both stark and fair.

Chimneys adorned in a snowy embrace,

As rooftops glisten with the season's grace.

A quietude settles over the wintry scene,

Enveloping the world in a serene dream.

Icicles dangle from the eaves above,

As snow-covered rooftops embody a love

For the wintry landscape, both bold and bright,

Guiding the world through the frosty night.

Joyful Moments

Through the wintry veil, a joyful embrace,
Moments dance freely, full of grace.
Laughter twinkles in the frost-kissed air,
As merry hearts frolic without a care.

Children's laughter echoes in the snow,
Crafting memories, a delightful show.
Frosty breath mingles with their playful delight,
Enlivening the world with joy so bright.

In the heart of the season's tender hold,
Winter's joyful moments weave stories untold.
A tapestry of mirth, in the frost's embrace,
Enlivening the spirit, a dance in grace.

Footsteps

Amidst the wintry stillness, a path lies in sight,
Frozen footsteps mark the journey through night.
Imprints in the snow, a story unfolds,
Guiding the way through the frost's icy holds.

Each step frozen in time, a tale to be told,
Of a solitary traveler, brave and bold.
Crystals glisten, capturing the moon's soft light,
Enhancing the beauty of the wintry night.

In the heart of the landscape, where silence
prevails,
Frozen footsteps narrate their timeless tales.
A testament to courage, in the frost's embrace,
Guiding the way with each frozen trace.

Frosty Meadows

Across the wintry plains, where frost does spread,
Frosty meadows glisten, white and widespread.
Grasses adorned in a delicate lace,
A winter's touch, a gentle embrace.

Sunlight kisses the icy blades with care,
Creating a spectacle beyond compare.
A shimmering landscape, in the morning's light,
A breathtaking vision, pure and bright.

In the heart of the meadow's wintry hold,
Frosty meadows weave stories, brave and bold.
A portrait of resilience, in the season's grace,
Guiding the world through the frost's embrace.

Flickering Lanterns

Amidst the winter's hush, in the cozy abode,

Flickering lanterns cast a comforting ode.

Shadows dance upon the walls, soft and slow,

Illuminating the room with a gentle glow.

Their golden light, a beacon in the night,

Guiding the way with a tranquil delight.

Casting warmth and solace in the wintry air,

Flickering lanterns offer respite and care.

In the heart of the home's serene embrace,

Flickering lanterns weave tales of grace.

A comforting presence, in the frost's embrace,

Bringing light to the darkness, a familiar place.

homemade pies

Within the winter's haven, the kitchen alight,
Homemade pies bake, a delicious sight.
Aromas of cinnamon and apples in the air,
Filling the home with a tantalizing flair.

Flour-dusted hands craft each crust with care,
Filling it with fruits, a delightful affair.
The oven's warmth embraces each pie,
Turning simple ingredients into a savory high.

As the timer dings and the pies are done,
Families gather, ready for some fun.
Sweet indulgence fills the wintry scene,
As homemade pies bring moments serene.

Indoor Snowflakes

Within the cozy haven, snowflakes gently fall,

Adorning the home in a whimsical sprawl.

Delicate crystals, dancing in the warm light,

Bringing the wintry wonder, a beautiful sight.

Paper snowflakes twirl, crafted with care,

Creating a scene so light and fair.

Their intricate designs, a marvel to behold,

Infusing the indoors with a wintry cold.

As they sway and flutter in the gentle breeze,

Indoor snowflakes bring a sense of ease.

A touch of magic in the warmth's embrace,

Enlivening the space with a wintry grace.

Winter Mornings

In the quiet dawn of the winter's embrace,
Winter mornings awaken with a gentle grace.
Frost-kissed windows reveal a world serene,
As daylight tiptoes in with a soft sheen.

Breath rises in wisps in the crisp morning air,
Footsteps echo softly, without a care.
A hushed symphony plays in the wintry scene,
As nature awakens, in hues of evergreen.

The sun peeks through clouds, casting a gentle ray,
Unveiling the magic of a brand new day.
Winter mornings whisper of promises untold,
Enlivening the spirit, in the wintry cold.

Cozy Book Nooks

Nestled in the corners, where the winter light peeks,
Cozy book nooks offer solace for the meek.
Pages whisper tales of lands afar,
Enveloping the reader, beneath the wintry star.

Soft pillows and blankets, a snug embrace,
Creating a haven, a comforting space.
Imagination soars in the quiet reprieve,
As words paint pictures, easy to believe.

In the heart of the nook's tranquil hold,
Cozy book nooks weave stories,
both brave and bold.
A sanctuary of thought, in the frost's embrace,
Guiding the mind through an intimate space.

Comforting Soups

Comforting soups simmer, soothing the soul.
Aromas of herbs and vegetables fill the air,
Creating a haven from the season's cold stare.

Hearty broths and savory spices unite,
Bringing comfort and warmth with every bite.
Vegetables and meats, a nourishing blend,
Offering solace, from beginning to end.

Steam rises gently in a comforting swirl,
As ladles clink softly against the soup's gentle curl.
Each spoonful whispers of comfort and care,
Filling the heart with a warmth so rare.

Winter Gardens

Beneath the wintry sky, where frost does cling,

Winter gardens slumber, awaiting the spring.

Bare branches and twigs, a delicate lace,

Adorning the earth with a tranquil grace.

Sleeping buds and seeds lie buried below,

Dreaming of the sunlight's golden glow.

Snowflakes gently settle on the quiet scene,

Adding a touch of magic to the wintry sheen.

In the heart of the garden's tranquil repose,

Winter's essence weaves stories, from highs to lows.

A tapestry of resilience, in the season's embrace,

Guiding the world through nature's tranquil space.

Winter Shoes

In the winter's chill, where the ground meets frost,
Winter shoes tread, no matter the cost.
Lined with warmth, they brave the icy cold,
Guiding each step, both brave and bold.

Leather or wool, a sturdy embrace,
Protecting the feet with a comforting grace.
Laces and buckles secure the hold tight,
Ensuring warmth throughout the wintry night.

In the heart of the season's resilient hold,
Winter shoes weave tales, both new and old.
A testament to endurance, in the frost's embrace,
Guiding the way with each firm embrace.

Winter Rainbows

In the wintry mist and the sun's gentle ray,
Winter rainbows emerge, painting the day.
A vibrant arc in the icy sky,
A breathtaking spectacle, soaring high.

Snowflakes and sunshine in a whimsical dance,
Creating a vision of hope and chance.
Colors glisten in the frosty air,
A reminder that beauty is always there.

In the heart of the season, where frost meets light,
Winter rainbows shimmer, a wondrous sight.
A moment of magic in the wintry glow,
Enlivening the spirit, with a radiant show.

Scent of Snow

In the crisp wintry air, a fragrance so light,
The scent of snow whispers, pure and bright.
A delicate aroma, both chilly and clean,
Enveloping the senses in a wintry sheen.

Hints of frost and icy whispers unfold,
As the scent of snow weaves stories untold.
A touch of freshness in the frozen breeze,
Carrying tales of winter with ease.

In the heart of the landscape, where snowflakes
play,
The scent of snow lingers, a silent display.
A reminder of nature's art, pristine and fair,
Capturing the essence of the wintry air.

Baking In Winter

In the warmth of the kitchen, as snow gently falls,
Winter baking sings through the hallowed halls.
Aromas of cinnamon and nutmeg delight,
Filling the air with a cozy invite.

Flour-dusted hands knead dough with grace,
Crafting delights for every palate to embrace.
Pies and cookies, sweet and warm,
Baking memories that will forever form.

The oven hums with a comforting sound,
As treats within slowly brown and round.
Vanilla and chocolate, a symphony of taste,
Creating a sweetness that will never go to waste.

Knit Blankets

In the cozy corner, by the crackling flame,
Knit blankets weave a tale of comfort and claim.
Stitches of warmth, in every fold and seam,
Enveloping the soul in a tranquil dream.

Soft yarn entwined in patterns so fair,
Crafting a haven from the winter's cold air.
Each loop and twist, a labor of love,
Embracing the body like a gentle dove.

Wrapped in their embrace, worries unwind,
As knit blankets offer solace, one of a kind.
Their gentle embrace, a touch of care,
Shielding the world with a warmth so rare.

Passage of Winter

As the days grow longer, the chill subsides,
The passage of winter gently glides.
A softening of frost, a thawing embrace,
Hints of change in nature's quiet grace.

The snow recedes, revealing the earth,
A transformation signaling rebirth.
Streams trickle freely, the ice gives way,
As winter yields to the promise of May.

The trees sway gently in the milder breeze,
Shedding their wintry coats with ease.
A palette of green emerges in the land,
Signaling the passage with a gentle hand.

Hibernation's End

As nature stirs from its slumber deep,
Hibernation's end, it begins to seep.
A rustling in the woods, a subtle sound,
Awakening life from its wintry bound.

The bears emerge from their cozy reprieve,
Stretching their limbs, eager to achieve.
The world awakens with a gentle sigh,
As creatures emerge under the blue sky.

The streams gurgle with a newfound flow,
The forest echoes with life's vibrant glow.
Buds peek out, a tentative start,
As nature renews, with a beating heart.

Spring Approaching

With winter's grasp beginning to relent,
The promise of spring becomes evident.
A whisper in the air, a gentle breeze,
Hints of blossoms and leaves on the trees.

The sun shines brighter, the days grow long,
Nature stirs, with a joyful song.
Hints of green peek through the thawing ground,
A symphony of life, soon to be found.

Birds chirp merrily, in the morning light,
Welcoming the season, with all their might.
A vibrant energy fills the air,
As spring approaches, beyond compare.

Final Snow

In the quietude of the season's repose,
The final snow descends, as the winter slows.
A gentle blanket on the earth it lays,
A fleeting touch in its wintry phase.

Each flake a whisper of the season's tale,
Softly alighting, delicate and frail.
In the stillness of its graceful flight,
It paints the world in a shimmering light.

The land, adorned in a pristine gown,
Embraces the final snow, settling down.
A moment of stillness, a tranquil grace,
As winter's last dance finds its place.

Winter's curtains

Where winter whispers in its silent breath,
Curtains of snow weave a tale of depth.
Nature's delicate fabric, in shimmering white,
Drawn gently across the land, day and night.

Through the frost-kissed panes, a world in repose,
Winter's curtains embrace the earth in its glows.
A tapestry of silence, in the season's hold,
Enveloping the world in a tranquil fold.

Soft flakes tumble down, a choreography rare,
As winter's curtains weave dreams in the air.
A dance of frost in the pale moonlight,
Painting the world in a shimmering sight.

Snow Started Melting

In the quiet realm where winter once reigned,
The snow started melting, the ice unstained.
A gentle thaw in the wintry air,
Whispering tales of the season's fare.

Drip by drip, the icicles weep,
As the sun's warm rays slowly creep.
The landscape transforms, a delicate hue,
Revealing the earth, both old and new.

The rivers swell with the snow's release,
Flowing freely with a newfound peace.
A symphony of water, in the winter's hold,
Breathing life into the land, bold and cold.

In the heart of the thaw, a promise is found,
Of spring's arrival, with its blossoms unbound.
As the snow started melting, nature's grand show,
Brought renewal and hope, in its gentle flow.

Farewell Winter

Farewell, dear winter,

with your frost-kissed morn,

Your whispered tales and the grace you have borne.

In your icy embrace, we found solace and light,

Now, as you depart, you leave us in delight.

So, farewell, dear winter,

as you take your leave,

Your enchanting spirit in our minds we'll weave.

Till next we meet, in your snowy embrace,

Farewell, dear winter,

with your quiet, gentle grace.

Now as we part, with fond farewell,

In nature's realm, we'll always dwell.

For through these poems, we have known,

Nature's essence, forever sown.

With grateful hearts, we turn the page,

In nature's love, our souls engage.

And as we bid adieu, we say,

Nature's whispers, here to stay.

As you reach the end of "Winter Whispers," I hope these simple verses have transported you to the ethereal world of winter's enchantment. Through these pages, I've strived to capture the essence of the season's beauty, its quiet marvels, and the warmth found within its frosty embrace.

I encourage you to carry the spirit of these winter whispers with you, allowing them to ignite a newfound appreciation for the magic that resides in even the coldest of days. May they serve as a gentle reminder of the tranquility and wonder that can be found in the embrace of winter's delicate touch.

If you found solace or delight in these verses, I kindly ask that you leave a good review on Amazon and Goodreads. Your words will not only encourage other readers to discover the charm of "Winter Whispers" but will also warm my heart with your kind reflections.

Made in United States
Troutdale, OR
11/14/2024